Your Free Gift

I wanted to show my appreciation for your purchase so I have put
together a free gift for you!

The Top 10 Procrastination Excuses

Just visit the link below to access your free gift

https://hutch13.leadpages.net/procrastination-book/

I know you will love this Gift.

Thanks!

Michael Moses

Table of Contents

Introduction

Given all the recent advancements in this world that have made your life more connected and filled with unlimited opportunities, why haven't you seized the moment and created the life of our dreams? I have a one-word answer for you. Procrastination, It is the devil that seems to take away your drive to achieve those dreams that you have started to suppress in your mind thinking that they are not reachable. It has stopped you from being who you were always meant to be. That devil is sneaky and good at deceiving. But all hope is not lost. You can beat down that devil procrastination and live those amazing dreams you have for your future. Identifying procrastination in your life can be one of the hardest things to do. I said that this devil is a good deceiver and I mean it. You may not even know you are procrastinating because it has become a habit but once you learn the how and why of procrastination it will be like someone turned on the lights in a dark room letting you see where procrastination is in your life. Just seeing will not get rid of this devil but it is the first step. You need to prepare yourself for war and arm yourself with real solutions to defeat the procrastination in your life. I am going to give you some great solutions that you can use to help you win this war on that devil procrastination. Do you wish to defeat procrastination, become a productivity master, and achieve your dreams? Great, take this journey with me and put into practice what you will learn so you can conquer this pesky devil procrastination.

How and Why We Procrastinate

Procrastination, that thing you do when you *know* there is a deadline closing in. It is that tricky thing that convinces us to watch hours of Netflix, maybe play excessive rounds of video games, or take that extensive nap that you are aware wasn't necessary. Then the worst hits. The deadline is hours away and you have done nothing to prepare. Procrastination takes off leaving you with his good friends guilt, stress, and panic. Why do we do this? Why do we let procrastination do its work on us time and time again leaving us in that nail biting emotional turmoil? Do we enjoy using the common excuse, "I work best under pressure," or is it something deeper?

There have been multiple studies as to why procrastination happens. There has even been a variety of classifications for different types of procrastination! Don't worry, we'll take it all one step at a time.

The reason you procrastinate comes down to one very simple truth that needs to be acknowledged. Psychiatrist Phil Stutz puts it perfectly when he says, "you procrastinate because you are avoiding pain." Now bare with me. I'm not saying it's an actual physically agonizing one. Pain can be categorized as something that is simply uncomfortable. That intense need to avoid this discomfort is what many psychology experts believe is the reason procrastination has become such a common unhealthy life style.

Let's look at it from a bit of a different angle. Based off of this definition you could also say that procrastination is the act of refusing to leave ones comfort zone. I know what you might be thinking- but the things that we are putting off are things that can better our lives, get us ahead, and potentially make us happy! Why would you think of those things as painful or uncomfortable? The answer is simple. Even if the result might be positive and life changing, it is the fact that we might be changing our lives that can be considered painful! Even if ones present is less than ideal, it is what we know which makes it comfortable.

So how do we let it get this far? How do we allow ourselves to become procrastinators or ultimately people who push off bettering ourselves or seizing the day? Well like anything else we do, its a habit that was conditioned.

Somewhere, in your early years, there were factors that contributed to you adopting this behavior. There are several examples of this. The easiest one is that it was a mimicked condition. Growing up, if your parents tended to be of the procrastinating nature, there's a good chance you saw it and took it as a habit of your own. On the other hand, you could have had a mother or father, or maybe both, who were extremely controlling and monitoring your every move. To think that by being there to catch you or make your day for you is an expression of love is a common idea from parents. In reality, it is keeping you from learning how to fend for yourself. When the time comes for youngsters to enter the world (college) they will do it with little knowledge of how to regulate their lives causing them to be easy targets for the terrors of procrastination.

Then there's the young rebel approach. We learn to procrastinate as a form of rebellion in situations where there are very little other forms to rebel. This one can fall once again on the parents. If parents don't at least create an atmosphere of consequence then these habits can and probably will continue into adulthood.

Now that we've examined what procrastination really is and some reasons for where the condition for procrastination comes from, let's see what it can look like.

We have the avoiders who as we have already stated, are avoiding pain and discomfort and are pretty much crippled by the fear of success. The avoider carries with him a common facade that he shares with other avoiders. He would rather people think he doesn't want to bother himself trying instead of letting anyone guess he really just doesn't have the ability.

Then there is the "Thrill seeker." I put this in quotes because it is the form of procrastination that isn't true, but rather just a claim based off self deception. Those people who claim they push things off for the sake of the excitement, or that they work better with the pressure, have just successfully lied to themselves. In reality they fall in the same seats as the avoiders. The truth is the pressure doesn't make them work any better nor are they more creative with a deadline looming. Lastly, there are the indecisive procrastinators. You know, those people who can't make up their minds about a course of action to take. Therefore, because of the stress and pressure, they push it off. The Indecisive procrastinator has a unique hope to them. In pushing off the decisions there is a little piece of their mind that is waiting to see if someone else will take up the responsibility that they are refusing.

Not to worry. Even though we have a multifaceted issue, we have a series of methods that help you get rid of procrastination once and for all. You are probably most familiar with the advice of, "just get a planner and stick to it." You won't be seeing that in this book. After all, telling a person to just a get planner to solve their procrastination is like telling someone with a drinking problem to just stick to water. There are actual real solutions and we'll be starting with the ABCDE method.

Procrastination in Action

So, before we dive into the ways to go about getting rid of your procrastination habits, we should take a look at some of the greatest scenarios of procrastinators in action. This can be beneficial since we know just like anyone with a problem; procrastinators can have a hard time admitting it to themselves.

The College Paper

Your teacher has just assigned you a midterm paper. The thing has to be a sixteen-page, double spaced research project with at least forty sources and you have one month to complete it. You write it down in your planner, notebook, post it note, cell phone, whatever thing you use to keep tabs on the things you are supposed to get done.

You listened to the teacher assign the paper and you had all the best intentions at heart. *This time will be different, I'm going to get started right away, I am going to put this on the top of my list. By the time the deadline comes around I will be so relaxed and accomplished.*

The next day comes and you had some other assignments to get done. *The research can start tomorrow.* The next few days pass. A lot of things came up and I just couldn't get started.

The weekend arrives. *Well I want to relax and have fun and not spend my entire time working on papers.*

Monday comes around and you look at a few sources in the library. You can't resist opening your Facebook account or scrolling over to Hulu to watch some television shows. You end up doing nothing but goofing off on social media and having a few laughs.

The pattern continues until at last, it's two days until the deadline, you remember you have a huge paper to write and instead of facing it, you treat it like you bank account after a week on vacation; you avoid it like the plague because you are too scared to face it.

The stress however doesn't leave you. It keeps creeping and in the last twenty four hours you have a large coffee, a bag full of snacks, and a camp set up in the corner of the library working until the late hours to get it turned in.

Pushing off the Dream

You have wanted to achieve a dream. Since you were young, you thought about becoming a writer and even created the idea for the perfect story. You have imagined it, you have been excited about it, it's just the thing you would like to read yourself. You tell your parents you want to become a writer. They say that isn't practical. You'll suffer and you won't be able to make ends meat. You let the "practicality" take charge and so you decide to go to school for something safer. You still have the idea of that book in your head. There are classes to be taken, there are papers to be written, there are romantic mistakes to be made, there's a job to find, there's a loan to pay, there's a car to buy, there's a party to go to…

You have your home, you have the spouse, you have the job, you have the stable income, and that idea is still there, creeping in your head. You keep pushing it off. It isn't practical. It's already been so many years! *No one would take me seriously now. I'm not a writer. I'm a lawyer, I'm a technician, I'm a social worker, I'm a vet, I'm a waiter, I'm an accountant…. I can't possibly be a writer. What will people think? I haven't done it in so long it will probably be horribly written. What if I do it and give up my time from being with by spouse or friends and invest money into the project and no publisher wants it? What if I try my hardest and everyone just says "I told you so."*

No, I can't do that. I have too many responsibilities, I have too many people counting on me, I have too many things going right now, I can't be a writer. I just don't have the time.

A Typical Day

You have woken up and there is a list of things on the kitchen counter that need to be finished. It's your only day off. The washer is broken and you need to get someone to come and take a look at it. You need to cut the grass, you need to cook dinner, you need to do the dishes, you need to clean the living room, and you need to take the car into the shop.

You are not excited to do any of the things on the piece of paper. You make yourself something to eat and sit on the couch to watch some TV. The next thing you know it's noon. There's no food so you need to get groceries to cook dinner. Your friend calls and asks if you want to hang out for a bit. That sounds much better than getting started on the list. You come up with the great "compromise" to go hang out and take the car to the shop afterwards while you get the groceries.

You sit around at your friends house until five. You didn't realize how the time flew. The shop is closed and so is the repair business for the washer. You need to hurry up and get to the grocery store to make dinner.

The car is giving you some trouble on the way over and you start complaining and asking why something like that always happens to you.

You finally get home and you need to cook but all of the pots and pans are dirty. You forgot to wash them. You need to take extra time just getting everything you need clean before actually getting started on making the meal.

It's getting dark out. It's too late for you to cut the grass. Your family gets home to see nothing done and you in a state of frustration trying to get dinner served as fast as you possibly can. You're agitated and cursing up a storm unable to figure out why these things always seem to happen to you.

The Big Moment

You have been working hard for years to achieve your dream. You are inches from making it to the level in your career that you have always wanted. The only thing standing in your way is one project, presentation, report, or assignment that needs to be sent over to your superiors before officially giving you the title.

This is it. Make it or break it. You are excited and you have a few weeks to get everything ready. You are telling your friends and family that you are up for the promotion. You're already planning all the things you will do to celebrate, and all the things you are going to buy with the raise. Days go by. You still haven't gotten started. The date is approaching and you are partying more, you're not getting as much work done, and you've actually been late to the office a couple of times.

Your boss asks you about the progress on the assignment and you tell him/her that it is going great. You are getting nervous because you haven't brainstormed what exactly you are going to do or present.

The day arrives and you've put something together, but it isn't exactly up to par with what they were expecting. Nor is it what you know you are capable of. They break the news to you some days later that they've decided to give the job to someone else and that they wish you better luck in the future. You sit alone and convince yourself it's fine. You knew it was too good to be true anyway. There was no way you were going to be able to achieve all of that.

These are four cases where procrastination has taken victory. Each of our experiences with it might look different in some of the details, but the process is all the same. Let's dissect the circumstances and figure out how we can stop this from happening again.

The ABCDE Method

The ABCDE method is the first strategy we'll review for beating your procrastination. The idea to it is simple. The method is used as a means to fight against negative thoughts and shake off attitudes of pessimism. The method has also proved profitable when it comes to abolishing bad habits. Think about it. How many times have you found it extremely easy to criticize someone else's negative behavior or bad decisions? Curiously enough, whenever we're the ones having the negative thoughts or doing the negative action, we frequently fail to apply the same critical reaction. The ABCDE method is about teaching you to be able to put yourself in check when necessary.

A stands for adversity or the issue you are currently facing. In this case, your A is procrastination. Easy enough right? (B) is going to stand for your automatic beliefs about the circumstance. Now be aware, there is a significant difference between what we *think* and what we *believe*. To clarify, what we think are things we tell ourselves. They are the facts and ideas that float on the shallow end of the pool. What we *believe* takes a bit more swimming. We're not always aware of what we truly believe.

For example, we can say, "I think I deserve to be happy." If our actions counter this statement then it cannot be what we believe. If we continue to engage things that are negative, bring us to negative places, or cripple us then the *belief* is, "I don't deserve to be happy." Until you can sit with the silence and swim to the bottom to find out what your belief is in any situation, you won't be able to alter your reality. So sit with it. What do you believe about yourself and your issue with procrastination.

C stands for consequences. This is a big one. It might seem like an easy and obvious step, but the truth is, many of us omit it in our day to day lives which is why we end up reliving the same issue multiple times! Just as you need to sit and find your belief, you must sit and acknowledge the consequences of your behavior. When you can list them and see what your procrastination is costing you, you can begin to address this habit as the issue that it really is.

The D stands for dispute. Once you have acknowledged the issue, once you have recognized the consequences that this behavior and belief have created, you can begin to dispute, and argue against it. How do we do this? There are a few ways.

Begin to search for proof that can counter the belief you've adopted. Let's look at an example scenario.

So you procrastinate. That is our adversity. What is the belief that makes us do this? For the sake of the example let's say the belief is, "I believe I am not worthy of success." The consequence of this belief has been myself putting off my responsibilities, assignments, duties etc. to the point that I am losing opportunities and people are losing trust in me and my abilities. To dispute it, start and finish the sentence, *"This belief isn't entirely true because..."* Begin to take the steps to argue against it. Know that at first it might take you a decent minute to come up with something. You might even think of an argument but not really believe it as the words come out of your mouth. This is ok! Remember, the belief is at the bottom of the deep end of the pool. It isn't just going to float to the top and see its way out. The dispute phase is the learning how to go down in one breathe. It's the learning how to tread water while you catch your breathe before trying to get rid of what's on the bottom. It takes time.

Words are things. Don't just think you're disputes. Say them out loud, write them down, give them life and a place in the world so they can begin to reside in you as a new belief.

The last step letter of this method represents being energized. This isn't the letter you practice but rather the state of being that results from all of your work. Once your belief has changed it will begin to alter your state of mind then finally your behavior. Procrastination won't be something you will entertain because you have become aware of the consequences of it and know that is beneath your value and your belief of what you deserve. We are nothing more and nothing less than what we believe ourselves to be.

Use the ABCDE method to try and eliminate the habit of procrastination. It won't be an over night process but nothing worth the time ever really is.

Once you have reached the state of being energized, don't stop disputing! The funny thing about beliefs and mind sets is that they function like muscles; you have to keep using them to keep them strong. Continue to affirm your new beliefs by writing down five to ten sentences that support the new state you're in to avoid falling back into the same patterns.

Power of Getting Started

Here is one the tricky situations about procrastination. You want to beat it, you want to be better, and you want to shake the habit. When the moment comes to get started to get rid of it, you end up procrastinating defeating procrastination! What an ironic concept isn't it?

Remember that we mentioned procrastination is simply nothing more than the fear of pain and/or the uncomfortable. Try and imagine an event or an obligation that you think will cause you discomfort or pain. Let's look at an example.

You have been invited to a party at the home of your significant other. It is the first time and you are going to meet the entire family. You are anticipating the nerves and anxiety of meeting all of those people at once and you are in a storm of fear and discomfort (pain!) before the introductions have even begun. You see, it's the anticipation, the getting started, that is the greatest step at striking horror.

So how do we do it? How do we take the hardest step of getting started? Let's go over some techniques. First thing is first. You need to internalize a very important fact. "Anticipation of pain or fear is greater than the actual pain or fear." This is the ultimate truth! Let's go back to that party. You get there, get out of your car, you're sweating a bit, and you have been dress rehearsing this in your head for days. Fifteen minutes later you find everyone to be nice enough, letting you in on their conversations, and maybe even laughing at your jokes. The stress and discomfort of the anticipation was worse than the actual event.

I know what you're thinking, what if it actually did go horribly? Well, if it went bad then it went bad! The night still ended, you still went home in once piece, and somewhere down the road you will probably laugh about it. Once again, your anticipation of pain before even getting started was worse than the actual event.

Get into yourself and understand it. Your procrastination comes from a base of fear. That is what keeps us from putting off that paper, putting off that book we want to write, or putting aside going back to school. We fear the pain of failure. We fear the pain of being criticized or judged. This fear of pain keeps you from even walking through the door. Internalize, "my anticipation of fear and pain is worse than the actual pain and fear itself."

How can we put this into perspective so we might be able to take the jump?

Sit down and grab a piece of pen and paper. If you're a technology fan then use a computer- it makes no difference. As long as you are putting it all out there where you can see it and visualize it.

Write down the things you have to be doing or the things you want to be doing that you are procrastinating. Got them? Great. Now sit with each one and ask yourself, "What's the worst that can happen?"

For any hardcore television fans, you might think this is a jinxed question. Every time a quirky group of characters is debating doing something out of the norm or away from their comfort zone they ask themselves, "What's the worst that can happen?" and the scene jumps ahead to them sitting in the worst imaginable consequence.

Let's remember, that is television. Next I would like to point out the greatest error of those sketches; we never saw them actually address what the worst that could happen was!

Look at your list. Let's imagine it says, "Write the novel I always dreamed of." It's an item on the list you have been putting off for years. We know now that it's a fear of pain, a fear of the worst. What is the worst? "I write it and everyone hates it. I write it and everyone makes fun of my creativity. I write it and no one will want to publish it. I write it and it completely fails to sell." Maybe these things show up in your worst case scenario brain storming.

The next question is easy. "Can I live with that?"

You want to write the book because something in you has a story to tell. Can you live with the event that some people might tell you they didn't like it? Can you live with the event that there will be a long list of publishers who will say no? Can you live with that? I'll let you in on a secret. It's a trick question because the answer should always be yes.

Yes, of course there will be people who say they don't like it and that will sting, but there will also be many people who will enjoy your style, your expression, and your message. Yes, there might be a long list of publishers who will hate it and only one will say yes, but that one will be all you need to get your story out there.

Pain is pain. It never feels great but it certainly always passes. After you have gone through your list and you have figured out the worst that can happen and weighed if you can live with the consequences, you can face the start.

The beautiful thing is, once you've taken the first step, the ones to come only become easier. It begins to move like a train. Remember the guy horrified of meeting the relatives? After the first hello, the second could only be easier. How about seeing someone getting ready to jump off a cliff into the ocean? Horrified the first time but ready to do it over and over afterwards.

It's no different with procrastination. Take that first uncomfortable step and see for yourself it only gets easier from there.

80/20 Principal

Have you ever heard of the statistic that twenty percent of our countries population controls eighty percent of the wealth? This concept is attributed to the 80/20 Principal created by a man named, Jospeh Juran.

The creation of the idea stems from the theory that the majority of things that occur, or results that transpire, come from only a small portion (twenty percent) of what we do. Though the 80/20 principal is an economic and management theory, it has been greatly used to assist in issues and other circumstances much like our dilemma of procrastination.

The idea that twenty percent of the things we do greatly determine the majority of outcomes would mean that a very selective list of our actions actually matter. the 80/20 principal fits into just about anything. Think about it. You have over 200 friends on Facebook, but you probably only hang out with a handful. A portion of the time of your week goes to your job, which produces the majority of the funds you gain to live. That paper that you need to write (that really wouldn't take that much time) to get the grade for graduation is the ticket for employment. 80/20.

We procrastinate because of fear of pain. We are afraid of failing and we are afraid of receiving what it is we want. We fill our days doing other things that are meaningless to the outcomes our heart desires because we can't take the steps to investing those hours to the task.

The first thing you need to be clear about is what are your passions. What is it that you want? Please don't say money. Don't get me wrong, we need money to live but if you think money is the key to happiness then we need to press pause on this for a minute.

We know that through money we can establish the comfort and feed the needs that we have. In a sense this does in fact bring us a level of happiness. The next idea is that if we can obtain even more money, then we will be even more happy. This isn't true.

The reality is that we have some confused some words. Remember, words are things. We have to make sure we're getting the right ones. Money doesn't really bring us happiness but rather *Satisfaction*.

With money we satisfy our hunger, with money we can satisfy our ego, with money we can satisfy our human needs. That is all. The excess of it does not buy us extra comfort or contentment. No, happiness is a unique thing to capture that is different to all of us. We must make it for ourselves and it comes from feeding whatever it is our passion might be.

By using the 80/20 rule, taking notice and accepting that a small portion of our actions determines the majority of our results, or better yet, our happiness, then we must pay close attention to what it is we want to focus on.

The sad truth about us procrastinators is that our twenty percent goes to things that really do not matter. Things that only promote an eighty percent of dissatisfaction, unhappiness, and frustration. We need to narrow down our list to determine what it is we should really be focusing on. Too hard? No worries, there's fun and challenging activity to figure it out.

Write down fifteen things you like and or love to do. You don't need to put them in any ranking order, just list them. Done? Ok. Here we go.

Step one- Cross off three things from that list that you will never do again. Three things that you are sacrificing from your life to never engage.

Step two- Cross off three more things that you will never do again.

Alright we're down to nine things left. Take a deep breathe.

Step three- You guessed it. Give the axe to three more things. You should now be left with six things on your list that you love to do.

Step four- The last round. You are going to eliminate three more things, but instead of crossing them off, place a circle around them.

You should now be left with three activities or actions that you love. These three survived the massacre that took out twelve things you hold dear. Now, I'm sure the first two rounds were probably the easiest. Getting to the top nine might have been where it got a bit sweaty.

The things you placed a circle around are important. They're the things that almost made it. Reflect on why they were cut. Take a look at the last three standing. If you did this honestly with yourself, then you should be looking at your twenty percent. You should be looking at the activities that you should be focusing your time in order to produce more of the result that they create. These are the three things that you want to fuel your eighty percent. These are the things that in theory, make you happiest.

Since I have no shame, I will share my list with you.

1. Working out X
2. **Writing**
3. *Falling in love*
4. **traveling**
5. reading X
6. **making people laugh**
7. *listening to music*
8. going to the pool X
9. swimming in rivers X
10. cooking/baking X
11. *watching tv/movies*
12. Dancing X
13. Using the internet X
14. Playing video games X
15. getting a drink with friends X

The ones with an X are the ones that didn't survive, the ones in italics are the runner ups and the ones in the bold were my top three. The thing I noticed was that my runner up items are the things I do the most! They aren't the top three things I can't live without and they are the activities I most engage? What is that about?

When you look back on your list, take time to see if some of the things you crossed off were actually some of the things you do to procrastinate.

Now, the game was just in hypothetical. You're not really giving up twelve things you like to do. The point of the exercise was to determine what your hearts priorities are. When your day begins, these are the things you should be doing. These are the things you should be placing as the most important.

If your top three happen to be partying, playing video games, eating, sleeping, drinking, or anything of that nature, then we have to call Houston because there's a problem.

Your top three should be things that inspire you, make you feel fulfilled, and make you feel alive. If the top three aren't things of that nature then you need to do some searching for what your passions are.

In the meantime, be aware of 80/20. If your primary interests and actions revolve around things of a negative nature, then you shouldn't complain with the eighty percent of the results that they're producing in your life.

The Power of Accountability Partners and Master Mind Groups

In the last chapter we touched on having friends and loved ones getting in on your rewards. These people can be called "accountability partners." As said before, sometimes when it comes to kicking a habit or bad behavior, it gets easier to get by with a little help from your friends.

You need a support system to try and fight behavior that is being detrimental to you and your living. We know that there are tons of procrastinators that create these excuses for why they can't complete tasks on time. If you're someone living in those excuses you know that it's a tough cycle to break without having someone there to hold up the mirror for you.

So, first thing is first, who can we ask to be our Accountability partner? You could have more than one, this is true, but you need to find that one person who you can count on for the thick of it. Brainstorm who within your family or group of friends seems the most supportive, most willing to participate, and most of all, most in support of the change you are trying to make.

Don't give the job to the one who makes you laugh the most, or the one who you have the most fun with. That's not what we're trying to achieve here. Find someone who obviously doesn't have the issue that you're trying to beat. It needs to be someone who has discipline, strong work ethic, and isn't afraid to call you out on the excuses that you're making. In other words, the person you pick should be someone that you are prepared to get annoyed by.

It isn't easy changing and it isn't going to happen over night as great as your intentions might be. There will be times where your excuses are going to try and come to the surface when the video game is getting good, or the bed feels extra toasty, or the TV is playing something awesome. You accountability partner has to be ready to slap the nonsense out of you and snap you out of it. Be sure you're ready for that kind of a support.

If you're looking for something that might be more communal then you could try a Master Mind group. These are made of people who want to work towards a goal together and assist each other in that pursuit.

When it came to the accountability partner, I wrote it should be someone who does not suffer the same issue you are trying to overcome. This remains true. When it comes to a Master Mind group however, the rule can be omitted. When there is a group of people suffering the same issue and are willing to engage in an effort to help each other defeat the problem, then there is a better chance of having someone around that can provide positive influence when another might be lacking.

I'm sure you have seen something like a Master Mind group in the past. You may have even tried to participate in one. There could have been that time you and a group of your friends wanted to get beach body ready for the summer so you created a group to help inspire you for a work out. You could have made a group for the sake of getting a school project done.

The truth is you can create a Master Mind group for any goal. The important thing is that everyone in the group is looking for the same resolution. When it comes to procrastination being the issue, I can understand how a Master Mind group might sound like a recipe for disaster.

The important thing to keep in mind is to make sure you establish a platform of honesty and creativity with the other members. Each person can contribute something different to the overall mission of the group. Be ready to play devils advocate for others, be ready to be told things honestly from your peers, and be ready to rely on them to get through the difficulty of seeing passed your excuses.

Things to avoid when it comes to Master Mind groups is having it be run by only one member. Everyone has to feel like an equal participant so everyone can feel the weight of the responsibility to get others through their issue and to their goal.

Master Mind groups could be used for the sake of one individual. When discussing accountability partners we emphasized the importance of using the "one" person in the case that having a multitude of people assist you felt overwhelming. If you are comfortable and feel okay with the idea of having multiple people participate in your group, then go ahead.

However, just like when it came to the accountability partner, be sure that all the people in the group looking to help you exclusively are people that can call you out on things that you are doing, can be there to help you, and carry lives of their own where the issue of procrastination isn't a problem.

You might be asking why it is okay to have everyone be a procrastinator in the collective Master Mind group but not in the individual exclusive one. Well, to make it a bit easier to understand, would you ask a cat to participate in a group to help one fish swim? It wouldn't make sense. If the group were made entirely of water fearing felines then there could be that mutual support and understanding since they are all suffering the same issue. If you are the only one looking for the help and you want a group that will help you conquer it, it would be better to make the group one filled with individuals that can help you eliminate it by means of their expertise and personal knowledge. You could include one other in the group who has your issues, but the group is for the sake of helping you. It could turn into something for the pair. That's alright, you just need to be sure it's what you want and that it will work. The last thing you need is someone instigating your bad habit.

The 20-mile March

Some years ago, Two men named, Robert Falcon Scott and Roald Amundsen, engaged a race to reach the south pole. Their approaches, however, well calculated they thought they may have been, differed in some critical ways. Scott had the idea to march forty to fifty miles each day depending on weather conditions. If there was some difficulty in the environment they would walk very few miles and some days even none.

Amundsen approached the race with a different idea. Regardless of the conditions being rain or shine, he and his men committed to walk twenty miles every day no matter what. Any guess as to who reached the south pole first?

If you guessed Amundsen you would be right. Sadly, Scott and his men not only lost that race, but perished in the seven hundred mile return trip. What lessons does the twenty-mile march principal teach us?

Let's take a look at the benefits of Amundsens plan first. By engaging the twenty-mile march plan he created clear and defined performance markers for his trip, he was able to calculate an exact time-frame for the entire endeavor, maintained a great sense of control over his missions, and of course, achieved his goal.

Now, perhaps you aren't planning on taking a march down to the south pole, but the 20-mile march principal is something that can be applied to every day life and the battle of beating a procrastination habit.

If we take a look back on Scotts approach, we can see very clearly that any sign or possibility of pain and discomfort (bad weather) would keep him from moving forward with his team. He would allow the elements that surrounded him to influence and overall make the decisions of when and how he would reach his goal.

We do this same thing when it comes to procrastination and our duties. We create a cir circumstance where other factors and obstacles determine when and if we are going to get our mission done.

We procrastinate because we fear pain. You must conquer this and Amundsen seemed to have pulled it off. Whether it was cold or raining he and his team stuck to the plan of completing their twenty miles a day. Hell, you could even call it their twenty percent.

Sometimes we look at our goals like a mountain impossible to climb. Where do we start? How do we even get started? What approach can I humanly take to even get this idea off the ground? It simply takes one foot in front of the other.

By keeping his daily distance to twenty miles, he was able to determine exactly when he would arrive at his goal and he knew exactly how to plan the day to day. He wasn't afraid of the discomfort. You can do the same. Think of your goal and construct your twenty mile march.

The secret to the success is simple. All of the elements of Amundsens approached focused around one element; consistency. To achieve the things we want we must be consistent in the pursuit.

If you want to be a writer, then make a limit of words a day you should be writing. If you want to have a great body, then set an amount of time a day you should be exercising, if you want to play an instrument then set up an amount of time each day that you should be practicing. Easy as that.

This is why it is so important to pursue the things that make you happy. Go after the things that make you feel fulfilled. The only way you are going to be able to master a skill or get to the place you want to be is by constantly practicing the art you want to perfect. Sometimes we procrastinate simply because the thing we have to be doing isn't something that we're interested in at all. It could be the assignments we have at the job we don't care for, or it could be the favor for someone who doesn't truly support us. The bottom line is that though I have said we can procrastinate the things we most want for ourselves from fear of having our dreams realized, we can also procrastinate the things that simply don't make us happy. Our passion should be something we want to engage without rest. It's that activity you do from the moment you wake up until the moment the night falls and you have failed to realize you didn't stop for a meal.

You might be thinking, "Well that's easy. If I really enjoy something of course I would want to do it! Why would I put that off or be inconsistent with it?"

Well, let's look back to Scotts approach to the race to the South Pole. Remember how he and his men wouldn't march if there were issues in weather or other uncomfortable conditions? Well, when we are pursuing the thing we love, the truth is we can come across moments where someone says we're not good enough at it, we should quit, we're being unrealistic, or we should stop while we're ahead. In other words, in the pursuit of our passion we can find ourselves all types of inclement weather conditions to make us stop the march.

Amundsen proved in his mission that it's no way to live. Slow and steady wins the race. You're in the chase of something new and unfamiliar to you. Let yourself have a couple of moments where you have no idea what you're doing. Let yourself have that moment where you make a mistake. Leave the umbrella at home and give yourself the freedom to have someone rain all over you with their words that go against your dream. Sure it'll be damp, but it's nothing you can't handle. Take your steps. Keep your twenty miles. Just go.

Celebrate Success and Reward Yourself

So, you've figured out your passions, you've taken the steps to get started, and your on your way to getting rid of your procrastination habit once and for all. This is great!
Now, there is that subtle worry going on in your head regarding how you will be able to keep this behavior up. Just like working out and getting fit we get concerned over if we will be able to keep up the routine and the new style of living. Not to worry. We have some ideas that might be able to help you stay on track.
We've talked about the idea of delaying gratification is a strong concept and practice of mature adults. But who are we kidding, procrastination is pretty much an illness and doing this can be very difficult! So we touched on the idea of engaging pleasure activities first for a set amount of time before getting into the things that we are avoiding.
Hopefully, if you have been using the ABCDE method and some of our other tips to get yourself focused, you should be adjusting relatively well to the practice of putting your responsibilities first. The key to keeping these practices in play is to create a reward system.
If you're like myself, you were a procrastinator at a very young age. My mother did what she could to try and knock it out of me by creating a reward chart. If I did said amount of things I could collect set amount of points that could earn me different rewards from the list I wrote myself.
This is an excellent approach, but no it didn't work. The reason was because I hadn't figured out any of the other important stuff first such as why I was procrastinating to begin with. The rewards idea can and should only be introduced after you've gotten yourself on a healthy track where your procrastination practices are fading away.

Now, the rewards idea can be tricky and tempting. If we have a list full of the lazy activities that we would throw ourselves into before we started fighting our habit, it could look like a smoker who has been without the stick for over six months creating a chart that rewards him with at least one pack of menthols. We must be careful!

Try and get a support system involved. Make some of the rewards something that you can't possibly give yourself. Get your friends involved! You love your aunts chocolate chip cookies. Have her agree to make it a reward after completing certain tasks. Certain things you like to do with your partner during private time, see if you can strike a deal! Make it engaging and make it something that you can involve others in.

Support systems are a key thing when it comes to beating bad habits and the rewards approach is a great place to get them involved.

The rewards angle can also be great for people who consider themselves to be competitive. It's a great visual for challenging yourself and reaching new heights.

Don't be limiting on your rewards chart either. Being bashful about the things you want to treat yourself to is just a sneaky trick your mind is playing on you to convince you once again that certain things aren't possible. If it's something you want, or something you want to do, put it on the list.

I'm going to get a bit cheesy for a moment and remind you, that the fact that you are beating your habit of procrastination, doing the things that you love without fear, and taking control of your life to see what you're worth are plenty of reward already!

When it comes to the reward approach, you hopefully won't be feeling guilty about treating yourself to things you like. Treating yourself is an important part of life and should not be absent as you move forward in eliminating procrastination from your routine.

There are also different ways you could approach the reward method. You could do it long term or you could even do it day to day.

Write down everything you are supposed to be getting done for the set day (hopefully full of your twenty percent) and for each task write a reward to go with it.

For example, you write down, "work-out for thirty minutes." To go along with it you write down "a smoothie" as a reward. You engage the activity and stick to it until it's complete and then you can treat yourself.

Sometimes, our list is full of daily activities that we loath. For example, it could be filled with things like, "Cut the grass, fix the washing machine, do the dishes," and other stuff that just makes us groan.

Don't get complaining just yet. Write these unpleasant tasks down and think of rewards that can really cancel out their negative effects. Or at least be positive enough to keep you neutral while you do them.

For cutting the grass I would write down a cold beer as a reward. For fixing the washing machine I would put down dinner at my favorite restaurant (regardless of price!). For washing the dishes I would put watching two episodes of my latest Netflix addiction.

See, just try and take the negative reaction that the task creates in you and think about something equal and opposite to go with it.

The truth is that there are so many things in our day to day life that we would rather not do. Regardless, they have to get done! Don't stay in the negative reactions they create. If your list is serving you tons of annoyance, just hit back with things you love. It's your life, you get to decide the tone of your days.

Take Time for Guilt Free Play

Procrastination has just about been exterminated. You're just about free from the stories of telling yourself you're not good enough and you've faced your fear of failure and discomfort. So, what now?

Have fun of course! We tend to focus at times exclusively on difficult matters and forget to enjoy ourselves. You might be saying, "But you said yourself that procrastination can be defined as avoid difficulty and staying in the comfortable and familiar." This is true, but at many times what we engage in our procrastination isn't necessarily fun, but rather numbing. It isn't giving us any real sense of joy or fulfillment but rather keeping us contentedly neutral. Remember the examples of procrastination at the beginning of the book? The things the people in those scenarios were doing to avoid their dream or responsibility wasn't making them happy, it was just keeping them occupied.

Fun can't be a constant. It's impossible. Fun is something we do to alleviate ourselves after long hours of hard work in the pursuit of our goal. Now if our goal is based off our passion, that in itself is a kind of fun, but we have to be conscious that breaks can be a good thing!

Take a look at your schedule and set a day of the week where you will not engage responsibilities. If you're feeling really in the zone, then fine, find a day for every two weeks instead. This will be your day to do anything else you want. Sleep in late, go see a baseball game, go to a water park, go for a ride on a bike, go hiking, do whatever!

Now, these guilt free moments of play don't only have to be condensed to one day.

The French say the key to pleasure and health is moderation. Remember in a previous chapter where we discussed creating a reward for every daunting activity you had on your list of things to do? Those are attempts at guilt free play! That is your making time out of your day to enjoy yourself and do some activities that you might not have done otherwise. Life doesn't always to have to be an uphill struggle or a list of chores and

responsibility after another. It can also be an accumulation of fun and enjoyment.

Don't feel guilty or bad about wanting to take some time to let loose and enjoy the success of your hard work! There are people who say constantly that life is too difficult to be alone. At the same time, life can also be too darn good to be alone! Find your friends. Find the people that support you and want to share in the celebration of your success. Surround yourself with the people that hope for you not to fall into the traps of procrastination. Those traps that whisper at you silently, "You're not good enough" and after you've gotten started and seeing the fruit of your work start to say, "Who do you think you are?"

Surround yourself with people that support your message of positive thinking and the space you've created of worthiness. Life is an experience to enjoy.

Dedicate yourself to your cause, to your passion, and defeat fear of discomfort and judgment. Don't be afraid to say you don't know how to do something or to try. Back in the first chapter we looked over the different classes of procrastinators. There was the "avoider." The person who tried to brush off giving his dream, responsibilities, or duties a try. He wanted people to think he didn't care when in reality he was afraid people would think he wasn't really capable of succeeding.

Guilt free fun can also be practiced even while you are engaging your goals. If you made a mistake, give yourself the permission to laugh. If you don't know what you're doing as well as the person next to you, make a joke and ask for their help. We are after specific results but the journey is just as important as any of it. The dream isn't later, it's now. After all, isn't beating procrastination learning to seize the moment?

Conclusion

Seize that moment!

Don't avoid that pain of being uncomfortable push through your comfort zone and see what all the world has waiting for you on the other side. Have faith and keep moving forward. That devil procrastination can't win if you are willing to take the time and energy to implement these simple tactics. You now know how and why we procrastinate. You have seen some examples of procrastination in action. Knowing the how, the why, and having examples of procrastination will help you to identify situations in your life where you are procrastinating but may not have really noticed or have been justifying it with excuses. If you haven't already, don't forget to get the free gift from me to you the "Top 10 Procrastination Excuses Identified". This gift will help you in your journey of identifying where that devil procrastination is sneaking into your life. Since knowledge is power you are know equipped to go to battle with and conquer that devil procrastination. But, don't forget that the journey is easier with comrades that have your back so make sure you go and find those comrades to go into this battle with together. Lastly remember to celebrate those successes and take the time to give yourself permission to have some guilt free play.

To your Success,
Michael Moses

Your Free Gift

**I wanted to show my appreciation for your purchase so I have put
together a free gift for you!**

The Top 10 Procrastination Excuses

Just visit the link below to access your free gift

https://hutch13.leadpages.net/procrastination-book/

I know you will love this Gift.

Thanks!

Michael Moses

Stop Your Procrastination Habits Now!: Become a Productivity Master to Cure Your Lazy Habits, Bad Patterns and Finally be Able to Get Things Done so You Can Live the Life of Your Dreams

By Michael Moses